Charles Dickens' London
1812 ~ 1870

by

Kenneth William Baxendale

A KL Litho Publication

DICKENS LONDON

Kenneth W Baxendale

First published, 1984

ISBN 0 9509802 0 X

A KL LITHO PUBLICATION

Published by KL Litho Ltd
Stapleton House 29—33 Scrutton Street
London EC2A 4HU

Typesetting by Triste Ltd Croydon Surrey
Printed by KL Litho Ltd

THE guard and Mr Weller disappear for five minutes: most probably to get the hot brandy and water, for they smell very strongly of it, when they return, the coachman mounts to the box, Mr Weller jumps up behind, the Pickwickians pull their coats round their legs and their shawls over their noses, the helpers pull the horse-cloths off, the coachman shouts out a cheery "All right," and away they go.

They have rumbled through the streets, and jolted over the stones, and at length reach the wide and open country. The wheels skim over the hard and frosty ground: and the horses, bursting into a canter at a smart crack of the whip, step along the road as if the load behind them: coach, passengers, cod-fish, oyster barrels, and all: were but a feather at their heels. They have descended a gentle slope, and enter upon a level, as compact and dry as a solid block of marble, two miles long. Another crack of the whip, and on they speed, at a smart gallop: the horses tossing their heads and rattling the harness, as if in exhilaration at the rapidity of the motion: while the coachman, holding whip and reins in one hand, takes off his hat with the other, and resting it on his knees, pulls out his handkerchief, and wipes his forehead: partly because he has a habit of doing it, and partly because it's as well to show the passengers how cool he is, and what an easy thing it is to drive four-in-hand, when you have had as much practice as he has. Having done this very leisurely (otherwise the effect would be materially impaired), he replaces his handkerchief, pulls on his hat, adjusts his gloves, squares his elbows, cracks the whip again, and on they speed, more merrily than before.

A few small houses, scattered on either side of the road, betoken the entrance to some town or village. The lively notes of the guard's key-bugle vibrate in the clear cold air, and wake up the old gentleman inside, who, carefully letting down the window-sash half-way, and standing sentry over the air, takes a short peep out, and then carefully pulling it up again, informs the other inside that they're going to change directly; on which the other inside wakes himself up, and determines to postpone his next nap until after the stoppage. Again the bugle sounds lustily forth, and rouses the cottager's wife and children, who peep out at the house-door, and watch the coach till it turns the corner, when they once more crouch round the blazing fire, and throw on another log of wood against father comes home; while father himself, a full mile off, has just exchanged a friendly nod with the coachman, and turned round to take a good long stare at the vehicle as it whirls away.

And now the bugle plays a lively air as the coach rattles through the ill-paved streets of a country-town; and the coachman, undoing the buckle which keeps his ribands together, prepares to throw them off the moment he stops. Mr Pickwick emerges from his coat collar, and looks about him with great curiosity; perceiving which, the coachman informs Mr Pickwick of the name of the town, and tells him it was market-day yesterday, both of which pieces of information Mr Pickwick retails to his fellow-passengers; whereupon they emerge from their coat collars too, and look about them also. Mr Winkle, who sits at the extreme edge, with one leg dangling in the air, is nearly precipated into the street, as the coach twists round the sharp corner by the cheesemonger's shop, and turns into the market-place; and before Mr Snodgrass, who sits next to him, has recovered from his alarm, they pull up at the inn yard, where the fresh horses, with cloths on, are already waiting.

The coachman throws down the reins and gets down himself, and the other outside passengers drop down also: except those who have no great confidence in their ability to get up again: and they remain where they are, and stamp their feet against the coach to warm them – looking, with longing eyes and red noses, at the bright fire in the inn bar, and the sprigs of holly with red berries which ornament the window.

But the guard has delivered at the corn-dealer's shop the brown paper packet he took out of the little pouch which hangs over his shoulder by a leathern strap; and has seen the horses carefully put to; and has thrown on the pavement the saddle which was brought from London on the coach-roof; and has assisted in the conference between the coachman and the hostler about the grey mare that hurt her off-foreleg last Tuesday; and he and Mr Weller are all right behind, and the coachman is all right in front, and the old gentleman inside, who has kept the window down full two inches all this time, has pulled it up again, and the cloths are off, and they are all ready for starting, except the "two stout gentlemen," whom the coachman inquires after with some impatience. Hereupon the coachman, and the guard, and Sam Weller, and Mr Winkle, and Mr Snodgrass, and all the hostlers, and every one of the idlers, who are more in number than all the others put together, shout for the missing gentlemen as loud as they can bawl. A distant response is heard from the yard, and Mr Pickwick and Mr Tupman come running down it, quite out of breath, for they have been having a glass of ale a-piece, and Mr Pickwick's fingers are so cold that he has been full five minutes before he could find the sixpence to pay for it. The coachman shouts an admonitory "Now then, gen'lm'n!" the guard re-echoes it; the old gentleman inside thinks it a very extraordinary thing that people *will* get down when they know there isn't time for it; Mr Pickwick struggles up on one side, Mr Tupman on the other; Mr Winkle cries "All right;" and off they start. Shawls are pulled up, coat collars are re-adjusted, the pavement ceases, the houses disappear, and they are once again dashing along the open road, with the fresh clear air blowing in their faces, and gladdening their very hearts within them.

Pickwick Papers

ACKNOWLEDGEMENTS

Dr David Parker, Curator
The Dickens House
48 Doughty Street London WC1N 2LF

Mr Cedric Charles Dickens
Author of Drinking with Dickens
and Dining with Dickens

Patricia M Baxendale

Dickens Inn by the Tower
St Katharine's Way London

The Old Curiosity Shop
13–14 Portsmouth Street
London WC2

Guildhall Library
London

The George & Vulture
See page 22 No. 49

This book
is
dedicated in gratitude
to my wife
Patricia
but for whose assistance
it could never have been completed

The Crooked Billet, King Street, Tower Hill
See page 22 No. 59

DICKENS INN by the Tower

St Katharine's Way London E1

Although Dickens Inn did not exist until 1976, we feel that it should hold great interest for all lovers' of Dickens.

A converted 18th century brewery warehouse, which lies at the heart of St Katharine's Dock, was reconstructed in the style of a balconied two storey inn of the Dickens period.

This historic part of Thameside East London was well known to Charles Dickens. In his *Sketches by Boz* he writes "One of the most amusing places we know is the steam wharf of the St Katharine's Dock Company on a Saturday morning in summer".

An ideal inn to stop-over for refreshment while touring Dickens London. *See map page 45*

Foreword

Cedric Charles Dickens
St Katharine's Dock, London
4 July, 1984

WHEN my great-grandfather was young, and writing the first paragraphs of Pickwick Papers, he noted that there still remained some old buildings "which have escaped alike the rage for public improvement, and the encroachments of private speculation." Charles Dickens was writing about old inns. *The White Hart* in Borough High Street, Southwark, where Mr Pickwick first met Sam Weller, the boots, disappeared at the end of the last century; but the *George,* in the next courtyard still survives, thanks to the efforts of the Dickens Fellowship and the National Trust. Today, alas, the *George* and *Vulture,* the old hostelrie where Mr Pickwick and Sam lived when in London, is at present under siege from those private speculators.

So it is going to afford a lot of people a lot of pleasure and satisfaction that Kenneth W Baxendale has shown such resource, sagacity and patience in researching the London of Charles Dickens and setting the results out in a way that He, who knew it so well, would have appreciated.

A lot of Dickens' London has disappeared — some of it badly needed replacing — but with these excellent maps in hand much of it can be recreated. You will spend many happy hours exploring my great-grandfather's London, and I hope that your knowledge, like that of Sam Weller's will quickly become "extensive and peculiar."

Cedric Charles Dickens

Introduction

THE DICKENS HOUSE

Charles Dickens (1812 to 1870) lived at number 48 Doughty Street from April 1837 to December 1839, not a long period but an important one, because it was here that he really secured his reputation. It is, moreover, the only London house still standing that this great London writer lived in for any length of time.

While at Doughty Street, Dickens finished **Pickwick Papers** (issued serially, like most of his books), wrote all but the first five instalments of **Oliver Twist** and all of **Nicholas Nickleby**, began **Barnaby Rudge**, and worked on such minor projects as **Sketches of Young Gentlemen** and **The Lamplighter** (a farce). He proved his talent to be not merely remarkable but durable, and he emerged from behind the *nom de plume* "Boz," into the blaze of fame that shows no sign of dimming today.

You may see the study in which the young writer, in his mid-twenties, created such immortal characters as Fagin, Bill Sikes, the Artful Dodger, and the Squeers and Crummles families. Today it is furnished with the desk and chair upon which he wrote such later masterpieces as **A Tale of Two Cities, Great Expectations** and **Our Mutual Friend.**

Before they came here, Dickens, his wife Catherine, their baby son, and Catherine's younger sister had been living in chambers in one of the old Inns of Chancery, Furnival's Inn in Holborn. This was their first proper house, and in it Catherine bore Dickens the two daughters who, with seven sons, survived to adult life.

But perhaps the most important thing to have happened at 48 Doughty Street, in terms of its effect on Dickens's imagination, is the death of his seventeen-year-old sister-in-law Mary Hogarth, of whom he was extremely fond. After a sudden and quite unexpected heart seizure, she died in Dickens's arms in her bedroom, which is on view, and her death left a deep mark on him. He remembered it, for instance, when writing of the death of Little Nell in **The Old Curiosity Shop** three years later.

Dickens as he appeared when living at 48 Doughty Street

Despite this sad event, good spirits prevailed for most of his time here, and Dickens began to be known for his genial hospitality. In the dining-room and drawing-room he entertained fellow writers such as Harrison Ainsworth, Leigh Hunt, Samuel Rogers and John Forster (later his biographer), illustrators such as George Cruikshank and H.K. Browne ("Phiz"), actors such as W.C. Macready and J.P. Hartley, artists such as Daniel Maclise and Clarkson Stanfield.

Visitors to the house may see portions of Dickens's manuscripts, letters, preliminary drawings by his illustrators, first editions of his books, including the original paper-wrapped parts, the desk he used for public readings of his works, the family Bible, and many other exhibits, including furniture, pictures, books and memorabilia. There are facilities for researchers, and the museum operates a Dickens information service for all inquirers.

In 1922, 48 Doughty Street, by then a boarding-house, was threatened with demolition. It was saved by the Dickens Fellowship, which raised money to buy the house, assembled the beginnings of a collection (since much augmented), placed it all under the care of a Board of Trustees, and opened it to the public in 1925.

If you are interested in Dickens and the Dickens House, the Dickens Fellowship could be the society for you. Open to all lovers' of Dickens, from the most light-hearted to the most learned, it is more than a literary society.

Founded in 1902, the Fellowship still concerns itself with charitable ends, though in Britain many of these are now achieved by the state. As a result, the emphasis has shifted to the study and enjoyment of Dickens and his works.

There are branches throughout the United Kingdom and the world, all of which are self-governing, fix their own subscriptions, and arrange their own programmes of lectures, recitals, excursions, dinners, etc.
Details are obtained from The Honorary Secretary, The Dickens Fellowship, 48 Doughty Street, London WC1N 2LF.

THE DICKENS HOUSE
48 Doughty Street London WC1N 2LF

MUSEUM, LIBRARY AND HEADQUARTERS
OF THE DICKENS FELLOWSHIP

(Registered under the Charities Act 1960)

Dr David Parker, *Curator, The Dickens House*

Charles Dickens' London
1812 1870
A
See page 13
B
See page 17
F
See page 33
G
See page 35
SOMMERS TOWN
PADDINGTON
HYDE PARK
GREEN PARK
St. JAMES'S PARK
QUEENS GARDEN
PICCADILLY
KNIGHTSBRIDGE
TOTHILL Fields
NEWINGTON
RIVER
SURREY
REACH
Battersea Common Field

HOXTON
HACKNEY
MIDDLE
BETHNAL GREEN
STEPNEY
LIMEHOUSE
ROTHERHITHE
DEPTFORD
KENT
THAMES
LONDON 20 Acres DOCKS
RATCLIFF HIGHWAY
COMMERCIAL ROAD
EAST INDIA ROAD
MILE END ROAD
OLD STREET ROAD
HACKNEY ROAD
New Road
Road to Oldford
C
See page 23
D
See page 27
E
See page 31
H
See page 39
I
See page 45
J
See page 49

(16) BROOK STREET. Where Mrs Skewton borrowed a house for Edith's wedding to Mr Dombey – *Dombey and Son.* Mr Dorrit stayed at a Hotel in Brook Street. – *Little Dorrit.*

(60) GROSVENOR SQUARE, Mews Street. Mr Tite Barnacle lived at No 24 – *Little Dorrit.* Lord Rockingham, Grosvenor Square – *Barnaby Rudge.*

(85) MONTAGU SQUARE. Mr Jorkins lived nearby – *David Copperfield.*

(95) PORTMAN SQUARE. The Podsnap family resided here – *Our Mutual Friend.*

(132) HYDE PARK PLACE

Map continued on page 17

Map continued on page 33

Scale 4¾ inches = 1 mile

Two views of Brook Street

Berkeley Square

Hyde Park Place

Grosvenor Square

(1) ADELPHI TERRACE and ADELPHI HOTEL. Mr Wardle's favourite stopping place when in London. Mr Pickwick celebrated here after his release from Fleet Prison — *Pickwick Papers.*

(4) BATTLE BRIDGE and Maiden Lane — *Dombey & Son — Oliver Twist — Sketches by Boz* 'First of May'.

(6) BELL YARD, Fleet Street — *Bleak House.*

(9) BLOOMSBURY SQUARE. Where Lord Mansfield's house was burnt by the Gordon rioters — *Barnaby Rudge* — also mentioned in *Master Humphrey's Clock.*

(10) BOW STREET POLICE COURT. The Artful Dodger — *Oliver Twist.* Barnaby — *Barnaby Rudge.* David's and Dora's page — *David Copperfield.* All taken to Bow Street Police Station. Bow Street is also mentioned in *Great Expectations* and *Sketches by Boz,* 'Prisoner's Van'.

(14) BRITISH MUSEUM — *Sketches by Boz* (The Boarding House).

(15) BROAD COURT — *Nicholas Nickleby.*

(20) CECIL STREET. Residence of Mr Watkins Tottle — *Sketches by Boz.* Charles Dickens himself lodged here in 1833.

(24) CLARE MARKET, site of The Old Curiosity Shop and the Gin shops 'among the handsomest in London' — *Sketches by Boz.*

(26) CLIFFORD'S INN. *Pickwick Papers — Little Dorrit — Bleak House — Our Mutual Friend.*

(27) CRAVEN STREET. Where Mr Brownlow spoke to Rose Maylie — *Oliver Twist.* Hungerford Market is also here where Dickens worked in the blacking house at Old Hungerford Stairs.

(28) CROWN INN — *Nicholas Nickleby.*

(30) CURSITOR STREET. Where Mr Skimpole took Mr Jarndyce, Ada and Esther Summerson to see Coavinses Castle — *Bleak House.* Mr John Dounce lived in Cursitor Street and Mr Watkins Tottle was confined in a sponging house in Cursitor Street — *Sketches by Boz.*

(33) DOUGHTY STREET, No 48. The headquarters of the Dickens Fellowship, a museum and library. This is where Dickens lived as a young man.

(34) DRURY LANE. Johnson's à la mode beef house, where David Copperfield ordered a small plate of beef. Dick Swiveller resided in Drury Lane — *Old Curiosity Shop.*

(35) DRURY LANE GARDEN. Poor Jo's churchyard, where Captain Hawdon was buried — *Bleak House.*

(36) DRURY LANE THEATRE. — *Nicholas Nickleby — Pickwick Papers — Uncommercial Traveller — Sketches by Boz.*

(37) DUKE STREET. Where Mr Twemlow's innocent piece of dinner furniture was kept over a livery stable-yard, when not in use — *Our Mutual Friend.*

(40) ESSEX STREET, Strand. Where Pip found a lodging house for Mr Provis (Magwitch) — *Great Expectations.*

(44) FOUNDLING HOSPITAL. Where Tattycorum came from — *Little Dorrit.* Founded in 1739 by Captain Thomas Coram. One of the conditions of this charity was that it not only educated and maintained the child but also reclaimed the mother. Handel presented an organ to the Chapel. Hogarth's painting of Captain Coram was also presented to the hospital.

(50) GOLDEN CROSS HOTEL, Charing Cross. David Copperfield stayed here and where he brought Mr Peggotty after the meeting on St Martin's steps — *David Copperfield.*

(51) GOLDEN SQUARE. Here lived the Kenwigs family, Newman Noggs and Nicholas Nickleby. Ralph Nickleby had spacious dwellings here — *Nicholas Nickleby.* David Copperfield and Martha found Little Emily in Golden Square — *David Copperfield.*

(52) GOWER STREET, UPPER. Where Mrs Micawber tried to start a School for Young Ladies — *David Copperfield.*

(53) GRAY'S INN — *Uncommercial Traveller — Pickwick Papers.* GRAY'S INN COFFEE HOUSE on the left of the Gateway where David Copperfield stayed when visiting Traddles. GRAY'S INN GARDENS, Flora and Arthur Clennam — *Little Dorrit.*

(54) GRAY'S INN, South Square, (Holborn Court). Where Mr Phunky had Chambers — *Pickwick Papers.* Traddles resided at No 2, Holborn Court — *David Copperfield.*

(55) GRAY'S INN LANE. Residence of Wilkins Micawber — *David Copperfield.* ACTON STREET was believed to be where Casby lived — *Little Dorrit.*

(56) GREAT MARLBOROUGH STREET, Police Court. Where Inspector Bucket started his search for Lady Dedlock — *Bleak House.*

(57) GREAT PORTLAND STREET. Mrs Briggs, her three daughters and two sons lived here — *Sketches by Boz.*

(58) GREAT RUSSELL STREET. Mr Charles Kitterbell lived here at No 14 — *Sketches by Boz.*

(68) HUNGERFORD MARKET. Mr Dick's lodgings were here over a chandler's shop — *David Copperfield.*

(69) INSOLVENT COURT and The Horse & Groom were both in Portugal Street, where the two Wellers met with Mr Solomon Pell — *Pickwick Papers.*

(71) KINGSGATE STREET. Where Mrs Gamp lived over Poll Sweedepipe's shaving establishment, next door but one to the celebrated mutton-pie shop — *Martin Chuzzlewit.*

(74) LEICESTER FIELDS. No 10 Green Street is believed to be the original Old Curiosity Shop.

(76) LINCOLN'S INN. Where the Lord High Chancellor sits in his High Court of Chancery. Here, the Jarndyce v Jarndyce case dragged on. Kenge & Carboy's office was in Old Square. Miss Flite lived close-by (see Sol's Arms) — *Bleak House.* Serjeant Snubbin had his office in Old Square — *Pickwick Papers.*

(77) LINCOLN'S INN FIELDS. Mr Tulkinghorn's house, No 58 — *Bleak House.* Aunt Betsey Trotwood stayed in Lincoln's Inn Fields for a week — *David Copperfield.* The Gordon rioters caused trouble here.

(84) MONTAGUE PLACE. Mr Perker's residence. Lowten came here with the news of Mrs Bardell's arrest — *Pickwick Papers.*

(89) NEWMAN STREET. Mr Turveydrop resided at No 26 — *Bleak House.*

(91) OLD BOOT, The. A lone house of public entertainment — *Barnaby Rudge.*

(94) POLYGON. Harold Skimpole lived here. An extremely dilapidated area. Many Spanish refugees walked about in cloaks, smoking small paper cigars — *Bleak House.* The Dickens family also lived here at one time.

(97) QUEEN SQUARE. Where Richard Carstone had furnished rooms — *Bleak House.*

(99) ROMAN BATH, Strand Lane. Where David Copperfield had many a cold plunge — *David Copperfield.*

(100) SACKVILLE STREET. Temporary residence of Mr and Mrs Lammie — *Our Mutual Friend.*

(103) ST CLEMENT DANES CHURCH. Mrs Lirriper's marriage took place here — *Christmas Stories.*

(107) SCOTLAND YARD. A very small tract of land where the original settlers were found to be a tailor, publican, two eating-house keepers and a fruit pie maker — *Sketches by Boz.*

(108) SERJEANT'S INN. Where Mr Pickwick was accompanied by Mr Perkins his lawyer, and Sam to Serjeant's Inn for the purpose of acquiring the necessary habeas corpus — *Pickwick Papers.*

(109) SEVEN DIALS. Dickens said: "What wild visions of prodigies of wickedness, want and beggary arose in my mind out of that place". It was near here that Nicholas and his sister Kate found Mr Mantalini being nagged by his wife to turn the mangle — *Nicholas Nickleby.*

Richard Carstone

Miss Esther Summerson *Miss Ada Cla*

Miss La Creevy

Mr. Joe Gargery

Mr. Abel Magwitch (Provis)

Map continued on page 13

Map continued on page 23

Map continued on page 35

Scale 4¾ inches = 1 mile

Seven Dials

(112) SOHO and SOHO SQUARE. A quiet area in Dickens' time. Carlisle Street, lodgings of Doctor Manette. In Soho Square Obenreizer lived with the beautiful Miss Marguerite and the mysterious Madame Dor — *Christmas Stories.* Also, where Caddy Jellby met Esther — *Bleak House.*

(113) SOL'S ARMS. Opposite Rolls Passage (Lincoln's Inn) is Chichester Rents. At the far corner stood the Ship Tavern, the original of Sol's Arms. Next door was Krook's Rag and Bottle Warehouse where they found Nemo dead. Miss Flite lived at the top of these premises — *Bleak House.*

(114) STAPLE INN. Where Mr Snagsby loved to walk in the summer — *Bleak House.*

(115) THE STRAND. Miss La Creevy, miniature painter, lived about halfway down the thoroughfare — *Nicholas Nickleby.*

(117) TEMPLE. Consists of the INNS OF COURT, (which number four). Inner and Middle Temple, Lincoln's Inn and Grey's Inn. And the INNS OF CHANCERY (which number nine), Clifford's Inn, Clement's Inn, Lyon's Inn, Strand Inn, New Inn, Furnival's Inn, Thavies Inn, Staple Inn and Barnards Inn.

(120) TOOK'S COURT, (Cook's Court). Mr and Mrs Snagsby, Law stationer — *Bleak House.*

(123) WHITE HORSE CELLAR, Coaching Inn. Mr Pickwick and Sam Weller took the coach for Bath — *Pickwick Papers.* Esther Summerson was met by Guppy at the White Horse Cellar — *Bleak House.*

(127) TAVISTOCK SQUARE. Dickens lived here from 1851 to 1860.

(133) BROARD STREET, SOHO where little Emily was found — *David Copperfield.*

Broad Street, Soho

THE OLD CURIOSITY SHOP

London's Oldest Shop

Dickens and the Old Curiosity Shop is an interesting pointer, as is the descriptive matter in the book itself. This gives a certain amount of information as to the location of the building which Dickens had in mind when he wrote the heart-stirring novel about Little Nell and the Grandfather.

In the opening chapters of the novel mention is made of walks in Covent Garden Market, but a few hundred yards from the shop. Again, describing the building, he says "a part of this door was of glass, unprotected by any shutter". The door and the removable shutter, mentioned later, is the same to this day.

A few paragraphs later on Dickens says, "preceding me with a light he led me through the place I had already seen from without into a small sitting room behind, in which was another door opening into a kind of closet, where I saw a little bed that a fairy might have slept in, it looked so very small and was so prettily arranged".

This room is used today as an office, but it is otherwise unchanged.

Dickens, with his unrivalled knowledge of the by-ways of London, would undoubtedly have noted this building, which even in those days was nearly three hundred years old.

Another interesting piece of local association is Dick Swiveller's remark which appears later in the book. He says "that while standing by the post at the street corner, he had observed a pig, with a straw in his mouth, issuing out of a tobacco shop." This tobacconist's shop and the post can be plainly seen in the illustration of the shop drawn above.

The statement at the end of the book that "the old house had long ago been pulled down and a fine broad road was in its place" can quite easily be put down to intelligent anticipation, for Kingsway was already being discussed, and eventually in 1905 this "fine broard road" was in fact constructed, clearing away a mass of old and slum property in the process. Kingsway was first planned to be placed a little to the east, and that would have meant the destruction of this charming old building.

In Portsmouth Street there were, at that time, no fewer than three pubs, one of which was the "Black Jack" renamed by Dickens in his book as "The Magpie and Stump", for it was here that Mr. Pickwick went to find Mr. Perker's clerk when the lawer himself was not to be found.

It was shortly after Dickens' death that Mr. Clayton Clarke, better known as "Kyd", whose illustration of Dickens' characters are well known, suggested to the proprietor that he should place under the inscription "The Old Curiosity Shop" the words "Immortalised by Charles Dickens".

The spirit of Dickens remains. The shop is still used for the same purpose as it was in the book, and all kinds of "old and curious" articles can be bought. The dividing partition between the shop and the sitting room has had to be removed; but otherwise the building remains the same as it was in Dickens' time.

Theatre Royal, Drury Lane

Gray's Inn, the Hall

Lincoln's Inn

Lincoln's Inn Fields
Home of John Forster, Charles Dickens biographer

Staple Inn

Inner Temple

(2) ALDGATE PUMP, Junction of Fenchurch Street and Leadenhall Street — *Dombey and Son — Nicholas Nickleby.*

(3) ANGEL, Islington — *Oliver Twist.*

(7) BISHOPSGATE STREET. Site of the London Tavern where the Company Meeting took place — *Nicholas Nickleby.*

(8) BLEEDING HEART YARD. Where the Plornish family resided, also where Daniel Doyce had his factory — *Little Dorrit.*

(11) BRICK LANE, No 160. The Brick Lane Branch of the United Grand Junction Ebenezer Temperance Association — *Pickwick Papers.*

(12) BRIDEWELL WORKHOUSE, House of Correction where Miss Miggs was chosen to be Female Turnkey for the County Bridewell — *Barnaby Rudge.*

(18) BULL INN, Holborn. It was here that Mrs Gamp and Betsey Prig nursed Mr Lewsome — *Martin Chuzzlewit.*

(19) CASTLE STREET, Holborn. Lodgings of Traddles — *David Copperfield.*

(22) CITY ROAD, Windsor Terrace. Where Mr Micawber lived — *David Copperfield.*

(23) CITY SQUARE. Approximately where the Cheeryble Brothers had their office — *Nicholas Nickleby.*

(25) CLERKENWELL. Gabriel Varden, the locksmith's house — *Barnaby Rudge.*

(29) CROSS KEYS INN, Wood Street.

(31) CUSTOM HOUSE. Peepy worked here — *Bleak House.* Also the late Mr Bardell — *Pickwick Papers.* Pip left his boat at a wharf near the Custom House — *Great Expectations.* Ralph Nickleby found premises in Thames Street for Mrs Nickleby and Kate — *Nicholas Nickelby.* Mrs Clennam's house was in this area and where Florence was found after having been robbed of her clothes by good Mrs Brown — *Dombey and Son.*

(32) DOCTORS' COMMONS. Where David went with his aunt for an interview with Mr Spenlow — *David Copperfield.* Jingle came here for his marriage licence — *Pickwick Papers.* Doctors' Commons is also mentioned in *Sketches by Boz* and *Little Dorrit.*

(38) EAGLE, The. Public House.

(39) ELY PLACE, Charterhouse Street. David Copperfield visited Agnes Wickfield who stayed here with the Waterbrooks — *David Copperfield.*

(41) FIELD LANE, Saffron Hill. Place wallowing in filth . . . Fagins's Den — *Oliver Twist.*

(42) FLEET PRISON. Where Mr Pickwick was imprisoned for refusing to pay the costs and damages to Mrs Bardell — *Pickwick Papers.*

(43) FOSTER LANE, No 5. Premises of Mr Chuzzlewit and Son — *Martin Chuzzlewit.*

(45) FREEMAN'S COURT. The offices of Dodson and Fogg — *Pickwick Papers.*

(46) FRESH WHARF. Mrs Gamp was looking for Mrs Jonas Chuzzlewit (Mercy Pecksniff) — *Martin Chuzzlewit.* Also mentioned in *Sketches by Boz.*

(47) FURNIVAL'S INN. Where John Westlock had rooms — *Martin Chuzzlewit.* Wood's Hotel in the Inn was patronised by Mr Grewgious who acquired accommodation here for Rosa Budd — *Edwin Drood.*

(48) GARRAWAY'S, the famous city coffee house. Mr Flintwich was a regular customer here — *Little Dorrit.* Also Nadgett, the enquiry agent — *Martin Chuzzlewit.* Garraway's is mentioned in *Christmas Stories* and *Commercial Traveller.*

(49) GEORGE & VULTURE INN. The Pickwickians stopped here before going to the trial at the Guildhall. Pickwick himself stayed here — *Pickwick Papers.*

(59) GREAT TOWER STREET. Joe Willet enlisted at the CROOKED BILLET in Tower Street as a soldier after a vain attempt to see Dolly at the Varden's house — *Barnaby Rudge.*

(61) GUILDHALL. The four Pickwickians came here for the trial of Bardell v Pickwick — *Pickwick Papers.* Jo Toddyhigh gave his description of the two City Giants — Gog and Magog — *Master Humphrey's Clock.*

(63) HANGING SWORD ALLEY, Whitefriars Street. Jerry Cruncher lived here — *Tale of Two Cities.* Mr George passed here also — *Bleak House.*

(64) HATTON GARDEN, No 54. The Hatton Garden Police Court — *Oliver Twist.* The Jellbys lived in Hatton Garden — *Bleak House.*

(65) HORN COFFEE HOUSE, 29 Knighrider Street. Where Mr Pickwick sent for a few bottles of wine while in Fleet Prison, to celebrate Mr Winkle's visit — *Pickwick Papers.*

(73) LEADENHALL MARKET, left of the market is Bull's Passage where the Green Dragon stood. Here, Sam wrote the famous 'Walentine' — *Pickwick Papers.* Sol Gills' premises were in Leadenhall Street. Captain Cuttle took charge of the Wooden Midshipman in Leadenhall Street. The offices of Dombey and Son were also here — *Dombey and Son.*

(79) LONDON WALL. Where Clennam and Doyce shared part of a house by London Wall — *Little Dorrit.*

(80) MANSION HOUSE.

(82) MINCING LANE. Bella Wilfer's father had his office in Mincing Lane in the name of Chicksey, Veneering & Stobbles. Mincing Lane had a distinct odour of herbs like a druggist's drawer — *Our Mutual Friend.*

(83) THE MINT or BANK OF ENGLAND.

(86) MONUMENT. Erected by Wren to commemorate the Great Fire. Charge of admission to walk up the 345 steps was 3 pennies.

(88) NEWGATE PRISON. Was destroyed by fire in the Gordon riots. Fagin died in Newgate — *Oliver Twist.* Kit Nubbles was imprisoned here for a while — *Old Curiosity Shop.* Magwitch was to face his trial here but death intervened — *Great Expectations.*

(96) POULTRY STREET, continuation of Cheapside, where the Military opened fire on the Gordon rioters.

(101) SAFFRON HILL, Little Saffron Hill. Mr William Sikes used to visit the public house called THE CRIPPLES. Fagin, Nancy, Noah Claypole and Charlotte also frequented the Cripples which was situated in the filthiest part of the street. Down St John's Road into Exmouth Street and Coppice Row, into a little court by the workhouse, across Hockey-in-the-hole, into Little Saffron Hill, then Little Saffron Hill the Great and at the bottom is Field Lane — *Oliver Twist.*

(102) ST BARTHOLOMEW'S HOSPITAL. Jack Hopkins was a student with slasher the surgeon — *Pickwick Papers.*

(104) ST LUKE'S WORKHOUSE. The Micawber's servant girl came from St Luke's — *David Copperfield.*

(105) ST MARY AXE. This is where the pretty roof garden was when Lizzie and Jenny Wren used to sit and talk above the premises of Pubsey & Co, presided over by Riah the jew — *Our Mutual Friend.*

(106) SARACEN'S HEAD INN and YARD, Snow Hill. Mr Squeers had his headquarters here three doors from St Sepulchre's Church — *Nicholas Nickleby.*

(111) SMITHFIELD WEST. Barnaby Rudge helped his father discard his irons after they had been released by the rioters from Newgate — *Barnaby Rudge.*

(118) THREADNEEDLE STREET. The Flower Pot Inn — *Sketches by Boz.*

(121) TOWER HILL. Residence of Mr and Mrs Quilp and Mother-in-law, Mrs Jiniwin — *The Old Curiosity Shop.*

Fagin *Mr. John Dawki (Artful Dodger)*

Oliver Twist *Miss Nancy*

Master Charles Bates *Mr. William Sikes*

Map continued on page 17

Map continued on page 27

Map continued on page 39

Scale 4¾ inches = 1 mile

Fleet Market (Farringdon Street) and the Fleet Prison
The old Fleet Prison was destroyed in the Great Fire, and like Newgate, its successor was attacked and burnt during the Gordon riots in 1780, but was at once rebuilt. It continued to exist until 1846. The site is now occupied by the Memorial Hall.

The Horn Tavern

The Racket-ground, Fleet Prison

The Old Saracen's Head, Snow Hill

Bleeding Heart Yard

(17) BULL INN. Aldgate Avenue was the site of the Bull Inn.

(110) SHADWELL. A month before he died Dickens paid a visit to an opium den in Shadwell accompanied by his friend, J.T. Fields. The den was probably in the vicinity of St George's church — *see Edwin Drood.*

(119) TITBULL'S ALMHOUSES — *Uncommercial Traveller.*

(125) GOODMAN'S FIELDS (Lemon Street).

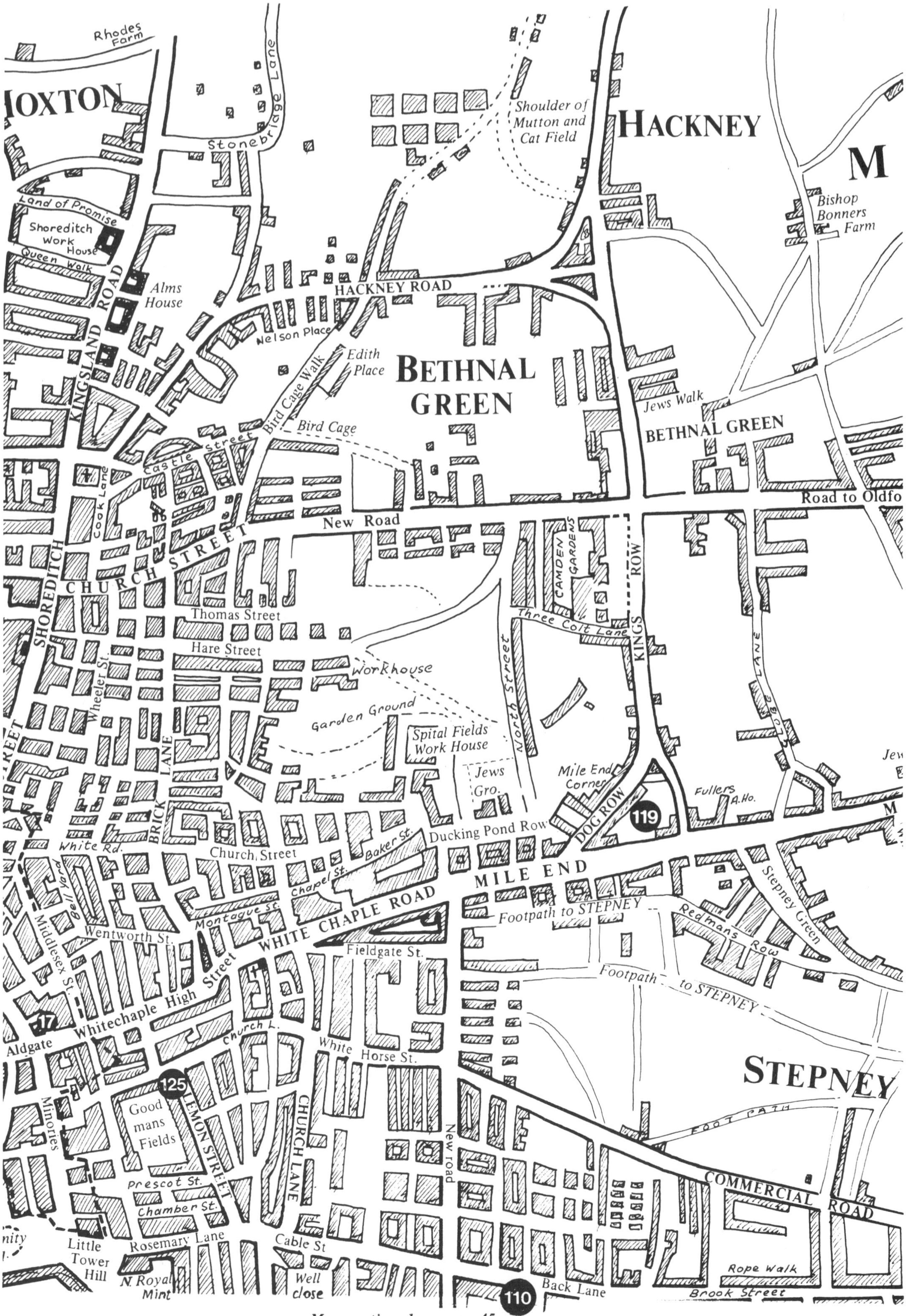

Map continued on page 23

Map continued on page 31

Map continued on page 45

Scale 4¾ inches = 1 mile

Goodman's Fields, Lemon Street

The Bull Inn, Aldgate Street

White Chapel 1837

Vintner's Almshouses, original of Titbulls'

The Six Jolly Fellowship Porters, Limehouse, taken from the original, The Grapes Inn

Limehouse Church

(75) LIMEHOUSE CHURCH. Lizzie Hexham lived in Limehouse, also Miss Abbey Potterson who was the proprietress of the Six Jolly Fellowship Porters — *Our Mutual Friend.*

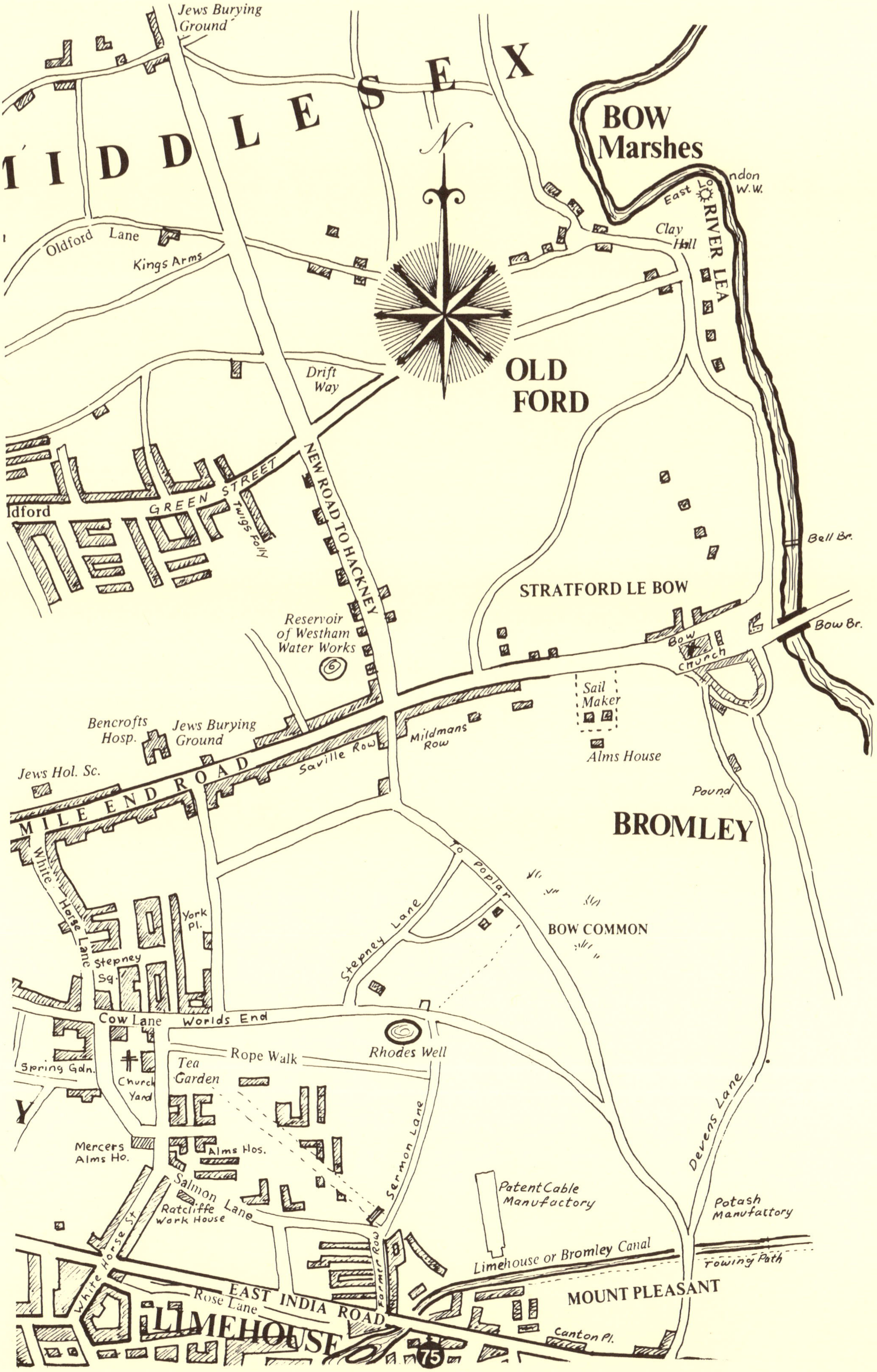

Map continued on page 27

Map continued on page 49

Scale 4¾ inches = 1 mile

St. Luke's Church, Chelsea

(5) BELGRAVIA. Lady Tippins' House—*Our Mutual Friend.*

(126) ST. LUKE'S CHURCH. Where Charles Dickens was married (April 1836)

(128) MRS WITITTERLY lived at Cadogan Place, Sloane Street. – *Nicholas Nickleby.*

(134) BUCKINGHAM PALACE. Where Dickens achieved the supreme honour of being received by Queen Victoria, three months before he died.

Map continued on page 13

Map continued on page 35

Scale 4¾ inches = 1 mile

Mr. Vincent Crummles *Newman Noggs* *Ralph Nickleby*

Mr. Pluck *Mr. Squeers* *Mrs. Squeers* *Miss Fanny Squeers* *Cheeryble Brothers* *Mr. Pyke*

Scrooge *Tiny Tim* *Bob Cratchit*

(21) CHURCH STREET. Where Jenny Wren the Dolls' dressmaker lived with her bad boy (drunken father) – *Our Mutual Friend.*

(87) NEW CUT, Lambeth. Where Joe Whelk lived – *Miscellaneous Papers.*

(92) PALACE YARD. Julius Handford (John Harmon) gave the address of Old Palace Yard to the Inspector at Limehouse – *Our Mutual Friend.*

(129) HORSE GUARDS

(130) ADMIRALITY

(131) LAMBETH PALACE

Smike *Nicholas Nickleby* *Mrs. Nickleby* *Kate*

Map continued on page 17

Map continued on page 33

Map continued on page 39

Scale 4¾ inches = 1 mile

The Queen's Palace, St. James Park

Admiralty

Lambeth Palace

Horse Guards

Little Dorrit Maggy Arthur Clennam Frederick Dorrit William Dorrit (Father of the Marshalsea)

Kit

Little Nell & Grandfather

(62) GUY'S HOSPITAL. Bob Sawyer was a medical student here and lived in nearby Lant Street — *Pickwick Papers.*

(66) HORSEMONGER LANE. Here John Chivery helped his mother in a tobacco shop — *Little Dorrit.*

(67) HORSEMONGER LANE JAIL, Session House and County Gaol — *Little Dorrit.* Dickens witnessed the last public hanging from the house opposite the prison.

(72) LANT STREET. Dickens lived here as a boy — Bob Sawyer also had lodgings here — *Pickwick Papers.*

(78) LONDON BRIDGE. Area where Nancy made her disclosure to Rose Maylie — *Oliver Twist.* Also features in *Barnaby Rudge — Martin Chuzzlewit — David Copperfield — Our Mutual Friend.*

(81) MARSHALSEA JAIL — *Little Dorrit.*

(90) OBELISK, generally called the 'Obstacle'. David Copperfield had his trunk and half guinea stolen and had to commence his journey on foot to Dover — *David Copperfield.* This area is called St George's Fields. The attorney's to the commissioners of the Insolvent Court generally had their residences within one mile from the Obelisk in St George's Fields.

(93) PENTON PLACE. Mr Gruppy lived at No 87 — *Bleak House.*

(98) QUILP'S WHARF (approximate area).

(116) SURREY THEATRE. Frederick Dorrit played a clarinet as dirty as himself, and Fanny Dorrit danced — *Little Dorrit.*

(122) VICTORIA THEATRE. Now known as 'The Old Vic.'

(124) WHITE HART INN and THE GEORGE INN — *Pickwick Papers — Little Dorrit.*

Mr. Brass

Miss Sally Brass

Daniel Quilp Dick Swiveller

Map continued on page 23

Map continued on page 35

Map continued on page 45

Scale 4¾ inches = 1 mile

The White Hart Inn and Tavern

Horsemonger Lane Gaol

The George Inn, before its alteration in 1889

Mrs. Crupp's residence,
York House, Buckingham Street,
(just off the Strand near Hungerford Market)
where David Copperfield lived – *see page 15*

The Surrey Theatre

Lant Street, Borough, where Mrs. Raddles let rooms to Mr. Bob Sawyer

The Marshalsea Jail

The Dorrits' garret in the Marshalsea Jail

Martin Chuzzlewit *Mr. Pecksniff* *Mr. Bailey* *Mrs. Gamp* *Tom Pinch*

Mr. Peggotty *Emily* *Mr. Dick*

Miss Betsey Trotwood

Mr. Pip Pirrip *Estella* *Miss Havisham* *Mr. Jaggers*

(70) JACOB'S ISLAND, (Folly Ditch). Home of Bill Sikes and where Sikes was hanged whilst trying to make an escape – *Oliver Twist.*

(135) DICKENS INN St Katharine's Way

Map continued on page 27

Map continued on page 39

Map continued on page 49

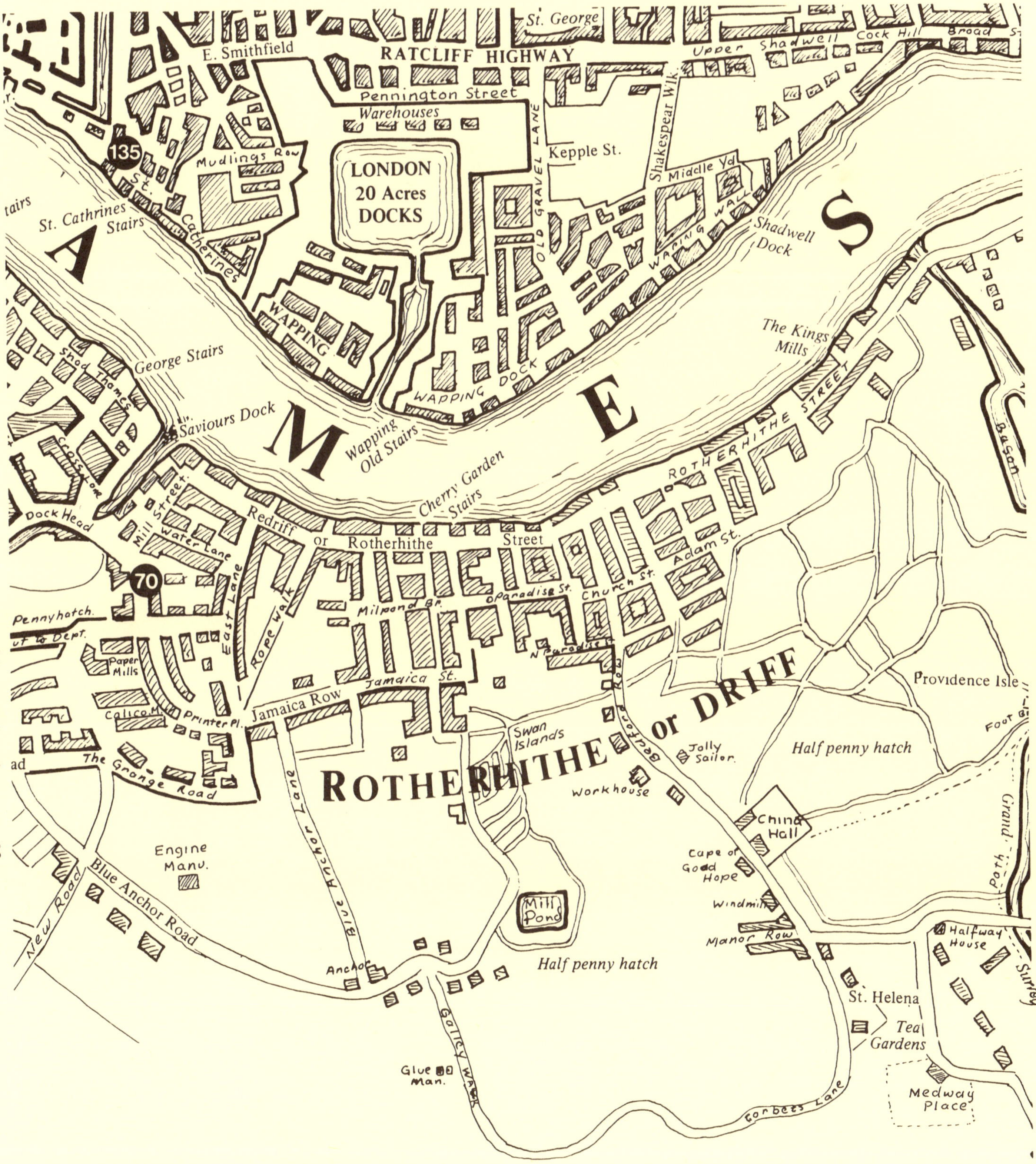

Scale 4¾ inches = 1 mile

Jacob's Island. South view of London Street, Dockhead, in the water side division of the Parish of St. Mary Magdalen Bermondsey

Old Houses, Jacob's Island

Charles Darnay — Mr. Lorry — Miss Pross — Mr. Stryver — Mr. Theodosius Butler (Edward M'Neville Walter)

Mr. John Dounce — Master Humphrey — Mr. Durdles — Toby Veck (Trotty) — Silas Wegg — Mr. Flintwinch

(13) BRIG PLACE, No 9. The approximate area where Captain Cuttle lodged with a Mrs McStinger — *Dombey and Son.*

Jenny Wren and her Bad Child

Map continued on page 31

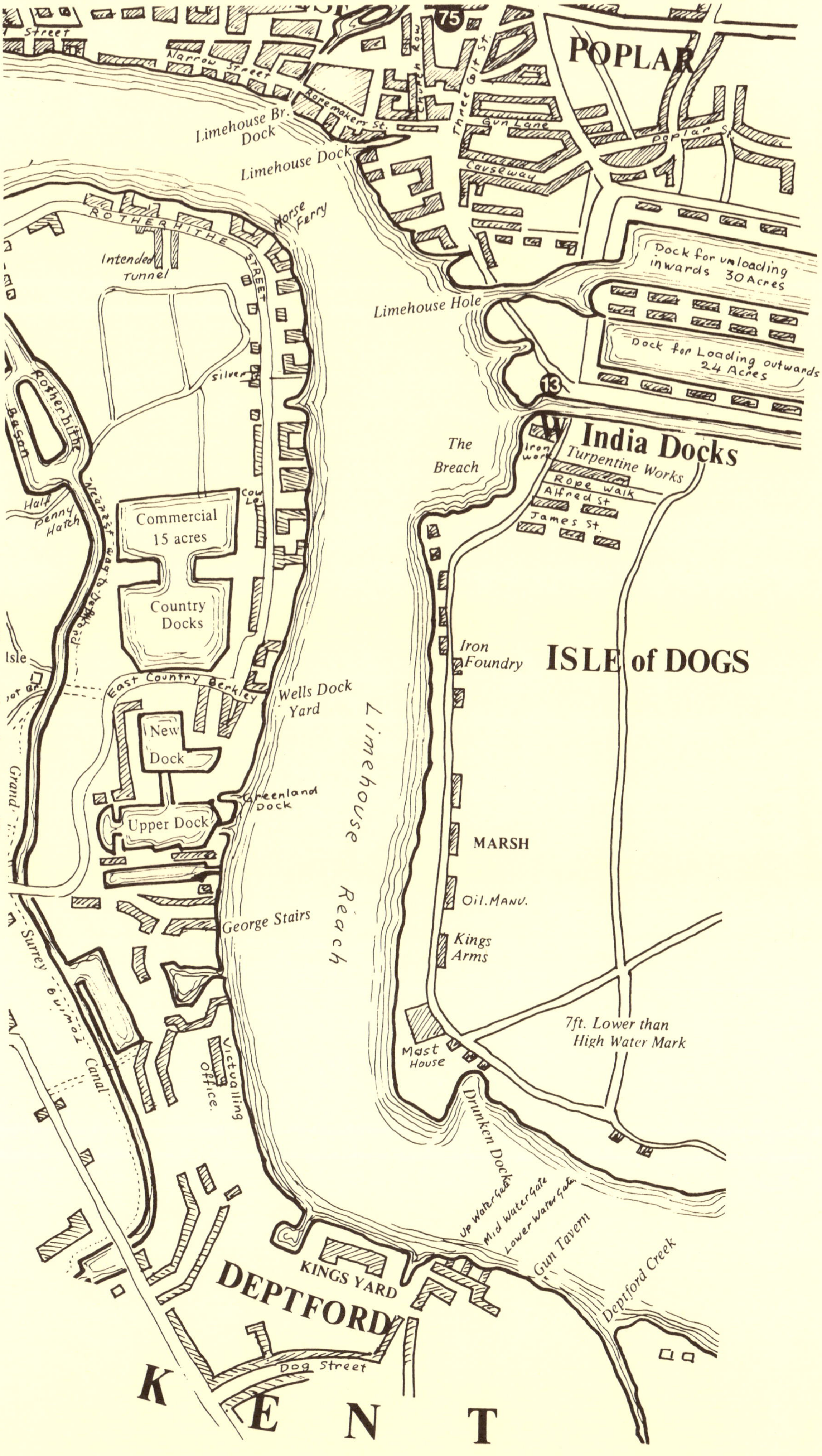

Map continued on page 45

Scale 4¾ inches = 1 mile

Entrance to the London Docks

West India Docks